All rights reserved. The scanning, uploading, and electronic sharing of any part of this book without express permission of the author is prohibited in accord with the copyright act of 1976.

Bumplovesme@Hotmail.com

ISBN-13 : 978-1-63553-000-1

COPYRIGHT 2016 by Brian Ahern
                          and Kathleen Dee Saville

BUMP!
Written by Brian Ahern
Illustrated by Kathleen Dee Saville

My cousin, Brian Ahern, from the Twin Cities has written a beautiful children's book addressing the issues of love and loss and the circle of life from the viewpoint of a little dog named Bump. She helps the family through the process of losing their beloved Grandma and "takes charge" to help them move on with their lives through the redeeming power of love - especially focusing on Grandpa.
    - Kathleen Dee Saville

This book is dedicated to my mother,

Phyllis Ahern,

who succumbed to Pancreatic Cancer,

and to all others who are dealing with the

devastating effects of cancer personally or indirectly.

Bump

runs!

Bump

jumps!

Bump

leaves carpets
in clumps.

Bump

gets excited when her favorite people visit.

Bump

brings gifts to
her friends.

Friends and family

love Bump.

Bump

loves her friends and family.

Bump loves tummy rubs.

"Don't stop!" thinks Bump.

Bump is helpful.

Bump cleans the carpet with her tongue.

Bump cares for and loves Grandma.

Grandma loves Bump!

Grandma always

wears her nightgown.

Bump sees something new.

Bump knows something is wrong.

Bump knows

something is wrong with Grandma.

Bump gives

Grandma extra attention.

Grandma

is in bed a lot.

Bump knows

where it hurts.

Bump crawls under the covers.

Bump is a lump.

Grandpa is sad.

The family is sad.

Bump

dances to make
them feel better.

Bump

brings them toys.

One day,

Grandma is gone.
Bump takes charge.

Grandpa needs her.

Bump waits under the covers for Grandpa.

Bump looks like a lump.

Bump makes sure

Grandpa goes to bed.

Bump and Grandpa

wake up.

Bump and Grandpa

are pals.

Brian Ahern grew up and still resides in St. Paul, Minnesota. The character of Bump is based on a real dog named Luna who gave unconditional love to two people struggling with end stage cancer. Future projects featuring Bump will explore Bump's early life as a shelter dog, Bump's experience finding the perfect family, as well as other topics inspired by Brian's experience with animals.

Kathleen Dee Saville was born and raised in the Midwest and studied Art at the University of Iowa. Kathleen has been a visual artist all her life, specializing in illustration, cartooning, and painting. She has been a public school art teacher for most of her career. She is also a musician who writes and performs her own songs. She is an accomplished illustrator for two previous published books. Kathleen currently resides in sunny Concord, California, where she never has to shovel snow.

www.ingramcontent.com/pod-product-compliance
Lightning Source LLC
Chambersburg PA
CBHW052045070526
44584CB00018B/2626